Barbara Hepworth What Do You See?

Laura Carlin

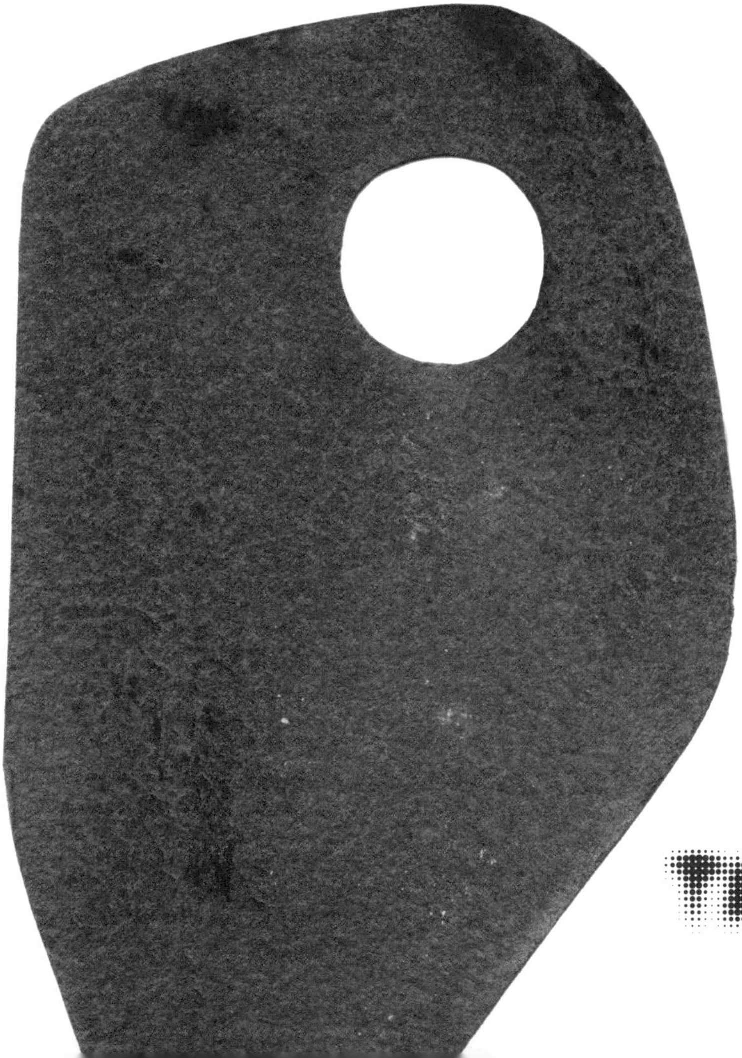

TATE

What can you see?
Can you see Flint?

No?
And Mrs Sycamore?

How about now?
(Whatever it is they're talking about, it looks pretty serious.)

From the age of seven, Barbara Hepworth saw the landscape made up of forms and textures. She saw the hills as shapes - sculptures - for her to make.

Because she looked at the hills and mountains around her for inspiration, Barbara's shapes are round and solid.

Lots of people find the shapes that Barbara made calming, whether or not they see a bird or a person or a landscape.

This makes sense because Barbara's love was for nature, people and for making.

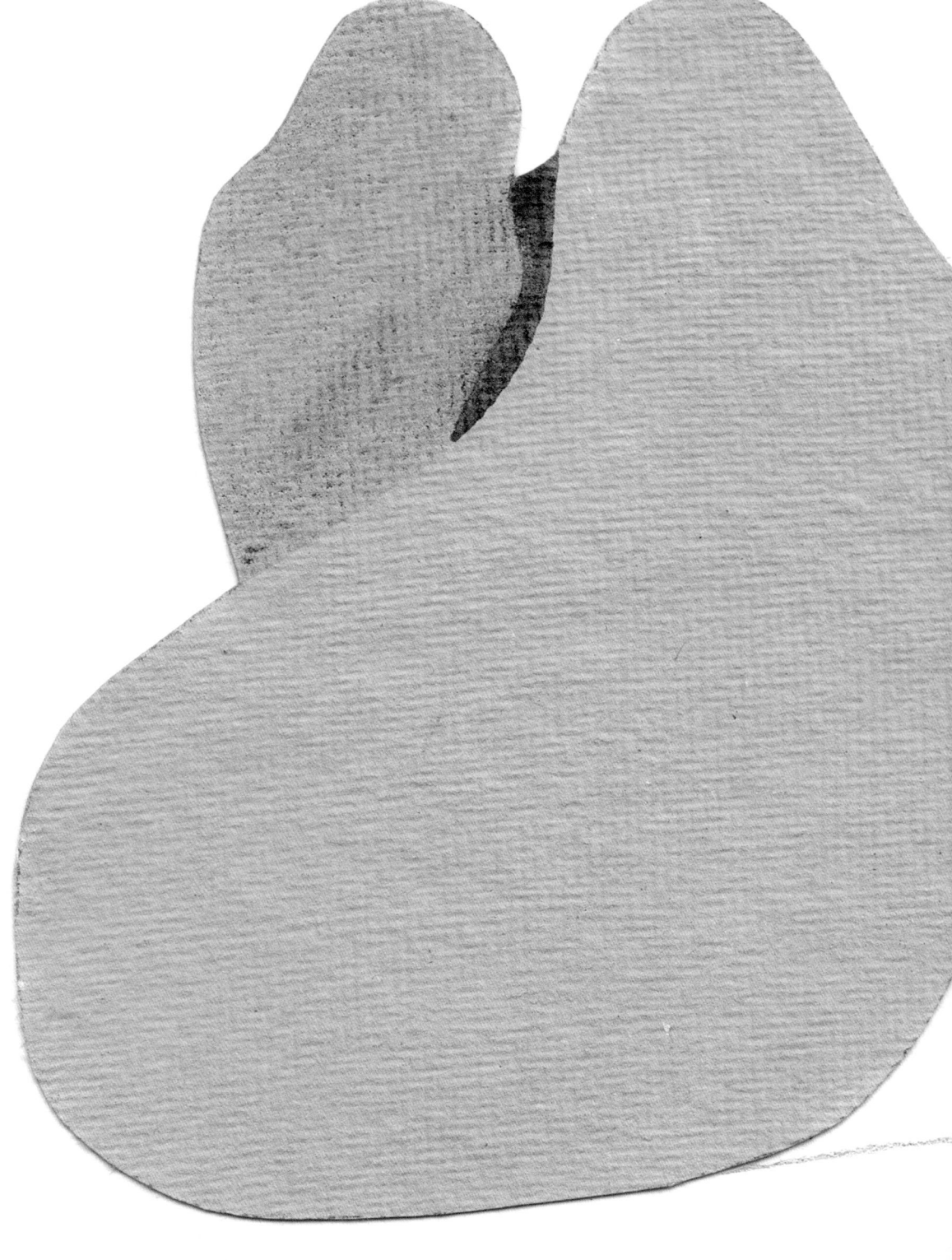

Barbara's figures started to talk to one another.

Then they started talking to everyone around them.

Depending on the space they're in, people move around the sculptures differently . . .

Barbara used lots of different materials to make her sculptures, like stone and marble, wood and bronze.

Can you find something to make your own sculptures with?

Are these materials hard, soft, rough or smooth?
Are they manmade or from nature?

Like Hepworth, you can look around you for inspiration.

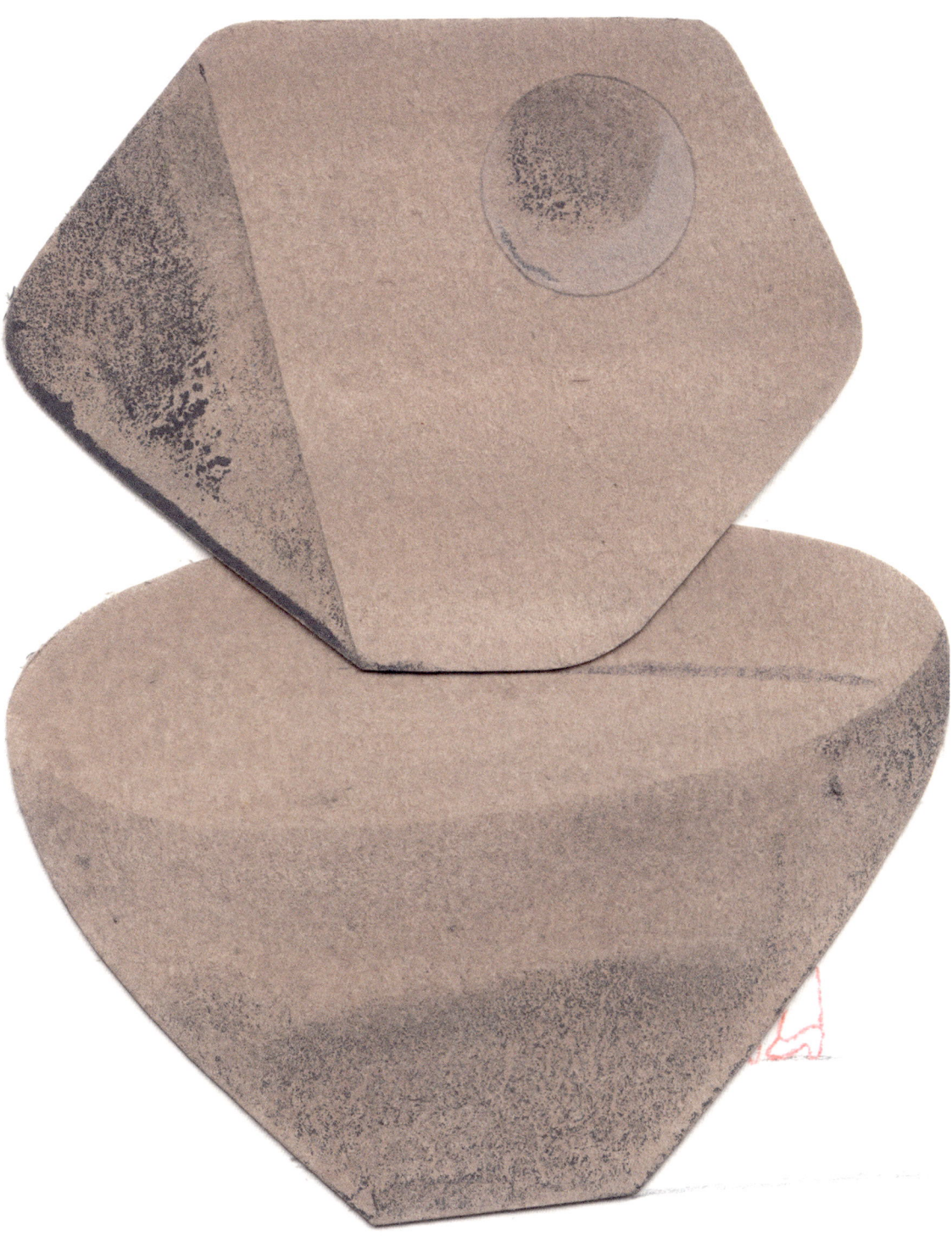

Think about how your sculpture looks from different angles.

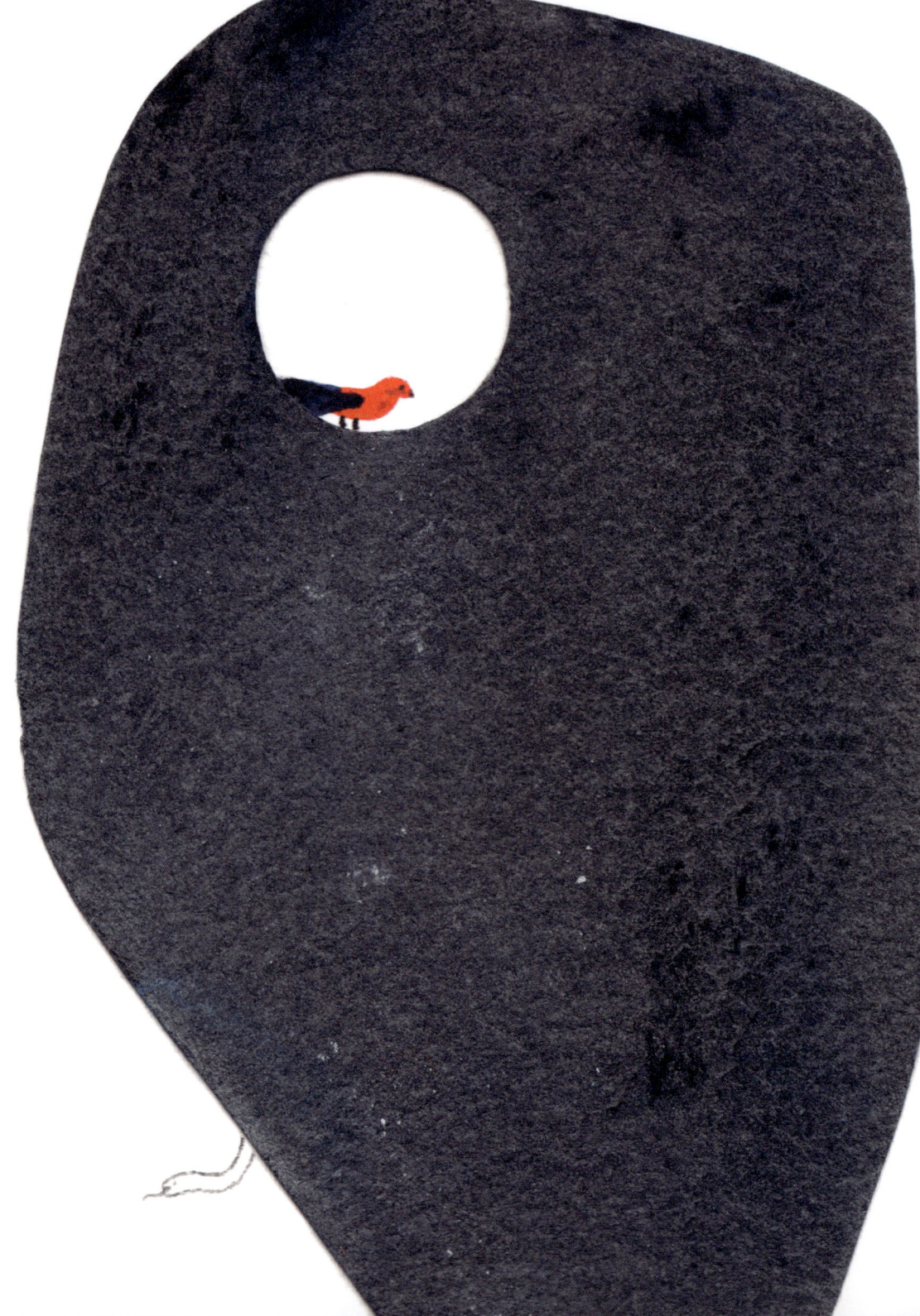

So, what can you see now?
What do you mean just a rock?!
Look closer . . .

And closer still . . .
What do you imagine is going on inside?
Who lives there?
What are they having for tea?

Some people just see a hole.
For Barbara, the hole was a
window into another world.

Who knows what you might see!

First published 2015 by order of the Tate Trustees by Tate Publishing,
a division of Tate Enterprises Ltd, Millbank, London SW1P 4RG
www.tate.org.uk/publishing

This edition published 2022

Text and illustrations © Laura Carlin 2015
All rights reserved
A catalogue record for this book is available from the British Library
ISBN 978-1-84976-785-9

Distributed in the United States and Canada by ABRAMS, New York
Library of Congress Control Number applied for

Colour reproduction by DL Imaging, London
Printed and bound in China by C&C Offset Printing Co., Ltd